SINGING IN THE CHOIR

A QUICK START GUIDE

By
Wayne Elliott

Make a joyful noise unto the Lord, all ye lands. Serve the Lord with gladness: come into His presence with singing!

Psalm 100: 1-3

Foreword

A Note to My Fellow Choral Musicians

You are reading this book because you probably want to be more effective as a member of your choir or chorus. Wonderful! That is my goal, too, for both you and me.

This is not a book about how to read music; rather, it will guide the reader in techniques of playing your vocal instrument (your voice) in such a way as to enhance the overall sound and message of your choir. This "Quick Start Guide" is intended to give you-- in short, easily digested bits of instruction-- some essentials. It is for the "church choir" because that is my perspective. Modern practices of worship and preparation for worship leave precious little time for the conductor or choir director, or whatever you call him/her, to teach techniques other than in the context of a particular musical piece and for a particular worship service. The vast majority of choir members are volunteers, and probably more than fifty percent already have had some musical training, but producing a pleasing "choral" sound has often not been the focus of that experience. Even wonderful soloists often are not very good choral members because the techniques of singing vary with the genres and with the number of performers.

In my mind, the choir should sound like one instrument, not twenty, thirty, forty, or more. Albeit, that instrument can produce chords, and the various parts of the chord can move simultaneously or at different times. By sounding like just one instrument, I mean that no individual voice, except in solo passages, should be distinguishable to the typical hearer, and that the parts of the chord should be appropriately balanced and blend well.

I know that you belong to your choir in order to worship, to lead in worship, and to have enjoyable fellowship as you craft your performance. With that in mind, I pray that God will bless you as you read and as you hone your talent.

Acknowledgements

Although the principles stated in my book define my default conclusions about how things should be done, I have endeavored to be technically accurate in every respect. Thus, I submitted parts of the manuscript to various people whom I considered experts or at least very knowledgeable about those parts, and I received useful feedback from all of the following. I wish to express my appreciation to Michael Cromwell, Kirk Elliott, Cheryl Elster, Randy Elster, David Scott, Karen Taylor, Kendall Taylor, and Ken Terrell.

The cover was developed in collaboration with author and teacher Josh Langston.

My thanks to my son, Scott Elliott for contributing illustrations, and to Annie Jefferson for supplying the back-cover photo.

The Crux of the Matter

Some essential rules

"Watch the director."

"Count."

"The first beat of each measure is always down."

"When possible, sing complete thoughts in one breath.“

"Listen to your director."

"Sing vowels tall, not wide."

"<u>Stay</u> at a given loudness throughout, until you receive a printed or a directed sign to change to a different volume .“

"Always listen for all of the parts."

Contents

I. Rhythm

I've Got Rhy . . . Rhy . . . Rhythm

Rule Number One: "Watch the director."

In choral singing, **"Rhythm"** refers to making sound *at the right time,* for the *right length of time,* and quitting the sound *at the right time,* as well as coming back in *at the right time,* if that applies. Thus, rhythm is a pattern of sounds and silences of various lengths.

When a group of people sing the same word, at the same time, and pronounced alike, how pleasing to the listener's ear it can be! More important, perhaps: that word can be understood. Members of the group may sing the same word, but if some start a hair before the others or hold on to it just a hair after the others have stopped, then the word may not be understood at all, nor will it be pleasing to the ear. (Pronouncing the word similarly is also a key, but that issue will be addressed later.) In my mind this, *rhythm,* is the number one problem that most church choirs have in being effective.

In First Corinthians 14: 7-9, Paul reminds us that we may have the most beautiful instrument in the world and know how to use it, but if it is not applied fittingly, for the benefit of the body of Christ, that sound is just noise.

So, how do we know when to start our sound, er..word? ***Rule Number One: Watch the director.***

Rule Number Two: "Count."

I am sure that you know that music has a beat, that music measures contain several beats, and that the choral director is waving his arms around in an effort to show you where that beat is. When the various voice parts are moving at different times, starting and stopping at different times, this can result in some pretty weird gyrations on the part of the director if he or she is trying to show each and every entrance and cut off for each and every part, making it nearly impossible to visually tell where the beat falls. This brings us to ***Rule Number Two: Count.***

The notes, themselves, tell you how many beats, or music pulses, to hold out the sound. You probably know that in music which is written in a way that a quarter note gets one pulse or beat, then a half note gets two pulses, a dotted half note gets three pulses, and a whole note gets four pulses. So, you simply count, or feel, the appropriate number of pulses then quit when you are supposed to, regardless of what the people around you are doing. This statement is an oversimplification because much music is written in a fashion that assigns one beat to something other than a quarter note, but the principle is the same, you must count the pulses and make your sound for the designated duration, then **quit.** Do not sing into a "rest." The silences are just as important as the sounds.

This statement borders on heresy, but groups can actually sing music without the aid of a Director showing you where the entrances and cut-offs are. It takes skill and artistry to do it right, but it can be done by counting.

Suppose that your director extends a hand or hands, and stops waving his arms...what does it mean? It usually means that he/she wants you to sustain the sound that you are making until he/she cuts you off. But, what if the *music* tells you that the note gets only three beats (or whatever number)? The director wins. The director always trumps the written instructions. Thus, ***Rule Number One: Watch the director.***

Rule Number Three: "The first beat of each measure is always down."

"The first beat of each measure is always down." That statement is in italics because it is a rule or axiom that is almost never violated by a good Director. In fact, where I studied music, I was told that every beat is down and that it is in

front of the Director. All of that other movement is either beat preparation or visual beat division. That works fine if you are directing hymns with a congregation or leading a waltz or march, but hardly any place else. There is far more to the interpretation of choral music than simply keeping a beat. Experienced directors vary widely and often wildly from that last statement. Just *remember the part in italics.*

Assume, then, that all beats are down. Where should your sound begin? Just before the hand reaches the bottom of the movement? Exactly at the bottom of the movement, or just after the bottom? Depends on which sound you are talking about: **is it the sound of a consonant or the sound of a vowel?** Most often, the open sound, that is the vowel, begins at the bottom of the beat and ends when you encounter the next consonant, or the next rest (take all of the rests), or a breath mark. Since the vowel begins at the bottom of the beat, any consonant that precedes that vowel must be pronounced just before the bottom of the beat, when the vowel sounds.

Rule Number 4: "When possible, sing complete thoughts in one breath."

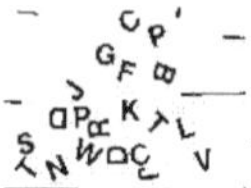 *Where did I put that last consonant?* This next principle effects not only pronunciation, but also rhythm and phrasing. Here it is: ***Whenever a word within a phrase ends in a consonant, and the next word begins with a vowel, tie the consonant over to the second word, so that there is no break between the consonant and the vowel.*** Two examples from "Lord of My Life": when the phrase is, "Lord of my life is Christ my King," "Lord" ends with the consonant "d", that consonant should certainly be clearly enunciated, but it should not be pronounced until just before the vowel, making it sound like "dahv." Then the word "life" (which has a silent "e") ends with an "f" sound, which makes the next word "is" sound like "fiz." This popular song is often sung as if there were a breath mark or rest after the word "life." (Director's option,

always) For the best effect, it should be sung as one unbroken, smooth thought.

Well then, suppose that the phrase is followed by a rest, rather than by another word. ***Hold the vowel sound for the full count of the note and do not cut off until the downbeat of the rest.*** Very, very important.

II. Phrasing

Mind your "Phrasiology"

Adapted from THE MUSIC MAN

Church choirs typically breathe every three or four words. This is the way that an average congregational member might sing. For the choir to be more effective than the average group of congregation members, some thought needs to be given to when and where you will breathe in order to get the message across clearly and to artfully express the music. Literally, we need to ***think*** about it ***before*** we get there.

In your hymn book, most hymns have one or two "musical phrases" to a line, and the same pattern is repeated line after line. The "musical phrase" is one reason why we in the choir tend to breathe twice every six or eight measures. It just flows with the music and feels right. This makes it easier for a congregation or other untrained group to stay together.

However, choral music, in order to be artfully and meaningfully expressed, requires that we breathe at the point that we might normally breathe if we were ***speaking***! That is, we should be singing entire thoughts and ideas (even when it includes carrying a sound over between the "musical phrases") before we take a breath, and we certainly ***do not*** want to breathe in the ***middle*** of a word. Do you do that when you are talking? I don't think so

Simple Example AMAZING GRACE:
Sing the entire first line without taking a breath: "Amazing grace: how sweet the sound that saved a wretch like me." For dramatic effect, some directors may want you to breathe after "grace." Never breathe after "sound" or after "wretch."
(Rule Number 1: Watch the Director)

Sing the second line, and so on, in one breath, i.e:

"I once was lost, but now am found." Could that be any easier? There are two musical phrases here, one ending after "lost," but only one idea. Do not breathe after "lost." Sing the idea.

Suppose that the director wants the choir to sing phrase, after phrase, after phrase, without an obvious breath being taken. What do you do? What you do not do is breathe at the most obvious places, no matter how tempting it is. But, take a discreet breath at really odd places when you think that your neighbor will breath someplace else. This is called "stagger breathing." Only your neighbor and perhaps the person in front of you should know that you took a breath.

III. Pronunciation

There is no "pronoun" in pro-nun-ci-a-tion)

Wha'd jew say?

Think about it, here in the United States, English is pronounced very differently from region to region. If you listen carefully, you may notice that it is pronounced differently all too often within a single church choir. ***How is the congregation or audience to know what you are singing?***

Easy enough. As a group, you simply **agree** to say each vowel and consonant the same way, and then stick to it. Fortunately, it has long been established by teachers of choral music that certain vowel sounds sing more freely than others and are understood more uniformly than others. These vowel sounds are: "Ah," "Eh," "Ih," "Oh," "Ooo," and sometimes "Uh." (There are several others, but let us keep this simple.)

I'll bet you thought that English vowels were the long "A," "E," "I," "O," "U," and sometimes "Y." Didn't you? Well, yes they are, but when we sing them they do not sound like that. For instance, say a long "A." and see if you catch the fact that it is really made of two distinct sounds. They are "eh" followed in speaking usually by a long "e." There are several problems that occur when you try to sing that. First, a bright long "e" sounds like dragging your fingernail across a chalkboard and causes the throat to squeeze off. Instead, that "e" should sound more like "ih." Second, does one sing both sounds equally long and loud, or should the "eh" be longer than the "ih," or possibly the other way around? *In general,* whenever the vowel is made of two sounds, the first sound dominates throughout until the very *last extreme fraction of a second,* when the second sound is *lightly* touched on. You didn't know that pronunciation could be so complicated, did you? Similarly, an "I" is really the two sounds "ah" followed by "ee," but sounds better when sung if you sing "ah-ih." Each of the vowels has its own quirky sound: the "O" is really "oh-oo;" the "U" is really "ih-ooo," and so on. How, then, are we in the choir to get together?

Rule Number Five:" listen to your director."

♪

I refer you back to those "singing" vowels: "Ah," "Eh,", "Ih," "Oh," "Ooo," and sometimes "Uh." One teacher, esteemed by me for his more than thirty years of musical training and experience, tells me that every vowel should be sung "as though you were singing, "ah." Is this getting ridiculous, or what? No, he is right, because he means that the openness of the throat and the placement of the sound within your head as it resonates, even when singing the other vowel sounds, should be as nearly like that of "ah" as you can make it. This will ensure the most comfort for you and the best projection of the sound toward your listener. While doing that, and singing the various vowels, form their sounds using only the sounds of the "singing" vowels referred to above if possible.

Think of singing each vowel *tall,* as opposed to wide. Doing so makes the "A" sound a little more like eh-ih than eh-ee. The same rule applies for all of the open vowels:

Rule Number Six:" Sing vowels tall, not wide."

♪

Singing pronunciation of the long vowels:

A eh-ee "Eh-ee" when spoken. "Eh-ih" when sung. The "ih" is not added until the last possible fraction of a second.

E ih As in "his," not as in "cheese."

I ah-ee "Ah-ee" when spoken. "Ah-ih" when sung. The "ih" is not added until the last possible fraction of a second.

O oh Open throat, round mouth, do not sing "uh."

U ih-ooo In this case, the "ih" is barely heard at the beginning. Again, sing with a round mouth and open throat. Sounds like "ewe."

Reading about making a sound different from the way that you usually do, will <u>not</u> cause it to happen. You must practice. Keeping in mind the things that I have just said, practice that way. Singing actually does take more effort than speaking. If you question a pronunciation, ask your Director. His/her instructions trump anything else. So, here is again ***"Rule Number Five: Listen to Your Director."***

Will that be with one syllable or two?

I really don't know enough about speech patterns of other parts of the United States to address them here, but here in the South, we tend to add syllables here and there, where they do not appear in the written word. There are far too many examples to name them all. For instance, in the word "lift," as in, "lift high the cross," some may tend to say "lee—uft," when there is really only one vowel in the word, and it is pronounced, in choral singing, as "ih." Thus," lee-uft high the cross" becomes "l-ih-ft" high the cross. "The principle is the same wherever we southerners tend to add syllables: ***if there is only one vowel present in the written word, then sing only one vowel,*** and there are too many such words to enumerate.

The "Rrrrrrrrr" Problem

One final note, so to speak, about pronunciation: Unless you are a soloist or sing in a very small group, nevah, nevah, evuh sing the letter "r" at the end of a word. A group of singers doing that sounds like a buzz saw. Instead, muster up your best London accent, where their pronunciation nevah ends with that "er" sound. Don't worry, the audience will never know; they will only know that you sound really good. "R"s also come sometimes at the beginning of a word or in the middle. There is a special way of sounding those without sounding like sandpaper. Here it is: Flick the tongue on the roof your mouth directly behind the teeth, just a little farther back than where you form the letter "d." When you do that, you will sound vedy, vedy good. (If the "r" follows a consonant, usually at the beginning of a word, the director may want you to either sound the "r" or to flick it.)

IV. Dynamics

"Dynamics" means "changes." The ebb and flow of things. In choral music, we are primarily concerned with two aspects of change: *speed* and *volume*.

"Tempo" is the term used to discuss speed in musical terms. For the typical choral singer, the tempo is set by the director and followed by the accompanist(s) and the choir. On the page, it is given in musical notation in numerical values for beats per minute, written above the music line. You may know what that means, but you do not have to: ***Rule Number One: Watch the Director.*** As the piece progresses there may be other terms above the music to change the speed: ***Watch the Director***. There are typically musical terms in Italian or abbreviated Italian which also indicate tempo changes. *Always be reading ahead* and, if you know the changes that are indicated be prepared to do them, but: ***Watch the Director.***

The **volume** markings are more familiar to most of us. When they are followed, the music comes alive with meaning. Follow those markings <u>unless</u> the Director decides to have you do otherwise. The markings vary most often from very, very soft **(*pp*)** to very very loud *(ff)*, and sometimes extremely soft or extremely loud (***ppp or fff***). Often the written Italian word will be given above the music as well, or instead of, these abbreviations.

Here are the corresponding notations, softest to loudest:

pp	very soft	pianissimo (This a virtual whisper
p	soft	piano
mp	moderately soft	mezzo piano
mf	moderately loud	mezzo forte (Think of this as the normal singing volume, then adjust all other levels to correspond relative to that)
f	loud	forte

ff very loud fortissimo

Crescendo and **decrescendo**, what do these words mean? Respectively, they mean get louder and get softer. They are often indicated by the written word or abbreviation above the musical staff. More often than not, however, these actions are called for by what appears to be an elongated bird's beak above the staff, with the point of greatest volume being at the open end. So, it could point either way, depending on whether you are supposed to get louder or softer. Get Louder Get Softer
Choirs tend to sing slower as they sing softer; *this is wrong*. Remember that the speed, or tempo, remains whatever is indicated and does not change with volume.

Rule Number 7: "Stay at a given loudness throughout, until you receive a printed or a directed sign to change to a different volume."

(This often requires considerable thought.)

V. Balance and Blend

Balance: When you sing with other voices singing different parts, you don't want to stand out like a sore thumb. However, there will be times when it is the role of your section to stand out above the others. In general, when a choir sings in four-part harmony, for instance, you want to *sing loud enough to be heard but not so loud that you cannot hear every one of the other parts as well.*

If you do that, the choir's sound can be said to be *balanced*.

How will you know when it is your section's turn to stand out? In general, again, your part will have a louder dynamic marking than the other parts. Those dynamic levels are different for a reason; observe them.

Suppose that all parts have the same dynamic level, are there times when one part or another should stand out? Yes! Some songs have the parts beginning phrases at different times. When it is your time to begin, sing a little louder, but watch to see when the other parts come in. When they do, back off a little, so that their part will be heard above your own. You may be surprised at how much more musical the piece sounds. This technique makes for beautiful interpretation, and the words and the meaning of the words will be so much clearer to the congregation.

Yet another time for a section to stand out is when your words are in motion while the other voices are not. The part in motion should stand out while it is motion, then lessen.

Rule number 8: "Always listen for all of the parts".

Blend: Breakfast Blend, French Roast, Columbian Blend, Supreme Blend may all be called coffee, and each is good in its own way, but they are slightly different from each other. Each voice in a choir, even singing the same notes and parts as you, may be good in its own way, but voice quality may differ so much from person to person that the combination may be distracting or even unpleasant to hear. You must put special attention to sound like one voice, instead of two, three, or however many. Each person's body is a musical instrument with a unique sound, much as a group of guitars may sound differently depending on size, quality and type of materials, and skill of the performer.

So what techniques may we use for blending? The starting point is to pay attention to the singer on either side of you and make your voice sound like one of theirs; they should be doing the same thing. Some voices may have a vibration (vibrato or tremolo) that is too extreme. With attention and practice, this can be lessened. Various voices may be characterized as strident, tinny, or scratchy, while others are more smooth and mellow. Other good starting points are to agree on how each vowel is to be pronounced. Then agreement in quality may partially be reached by where each person places the sound: whether in the throat, the chest, the front of the mouth or perhaps the sinus passages. In my experience, vowel sounds are easier to make and to control and are heard better and truer when the singer has both an open throat and mouth and then does his or her best to project the sound even higher in the head. Imagine singing through your eyes. **Your entire vocal instrument extends from the diaphragm (around the belly button) to your eyes.** The main thing is to listen and to make adjustments.

VI. So, Whose (De)fault Is It, Anyway?

It is your default. The techniques that I have attempted to teach in this book are my default settings. They are the methods that I intend to employ all of the time when singing in a choir, unless the director has other ideas.

If you were a dancer, you might first learn the dance steps, think about them, practice them, correct them, practice some more, and internalize them so that at performance time you simply do them, by default. An athlete might first learn what to do, then practice over and over and make corrections, then at game time just do it, because "that is how is done," by default.

My default decisions, for that is what these techniques are, are the ones that I have learned over a lifetime, since the age of six, of singing almost continually in church choirs and a community chorus, and from majoring in

Church Music in my college days. As of now, I have the privilege of learning from five different directors as I participate in my church choir and in The Georgia Festival Chorus. Perhaps my directors have hoped that I might learn more or something different; nevertheless, what I have presented here are my default settings.

My fervent desire is that you will continue always to hone the musical gift that is yours and to develop your own default settings, so that you will employ them as the natural thing to do, ***unless your director tells you otherwise.*** If your choral director is not in sync with what you believe to be good technique, go with him/her for the good of your group unless it makes you too uncomfortable. In which case, you might consider finding a different choir to belong to.

I wish you joy and happy singing!

Let the word of Christ dwell in you richly in all wisdom: teaching and admonishing one another in psalms and hymns and in spiritual songs, singing with grace in your hearts to the Lord. Colossians 3:16

27595648R00022

Made in the USA
Lexington, KY
05 January 2019